Science
Vocabulary Readers

Chick
Life Cycle

Elizabeth Bennett

SCHOLASTIC INC.

NEW YORK • TORONTO • LONDON • AUCKLAND • SYDNEY
MEXICO CITY • NEW DELHI • HONG KONG • BUENOS AIRES

ISBN: 978-0-439-87658-2

Photos Credits:

Cover: © DV/Getty Images; title page: © Julie Habel/Corbis; contents page, from top: © Bruce Coleman USA Inc., © Ullstein-Klein/Peter Arnold, Inc., © Heidi & Hans-Jurgen Koch/Minden Pictures, © Getty Images; page 4: © Bruce Coleman USA Inc.; page 5, top: © Chase Swift/Corbis; page 5, bottom: © Getty Images; page 6, top right: © Getty Images; page 6, bottom left: © Robert Dowling/Corbis; page 6, bottom right: © Robert Dowling/Corbis; page 7, top left: © Getty Images; page 7, top right: © Robert Dowling/Corbis; page 7, bottom left: © Getty Images; page 7, bottom right: © Robert Dowling/Corbis; page 8: © Robert Dowling/Corbis; page 9: © Lynn D. Odell/Animals Animals; page 10: © Dwight Kuhn Photography; page 11: © Ullstein-Klein/Peter Arnold, Inc.; page 12, left: © Robert Pickett/Corbis; page 12, right: © Dwight Kuhn Photography; page 13, left: © Dwight Kuhn Photography; page 13, right: © Robert Pickett/Corbis; page 14: © Getty Images; page 15: © Heidi & Hans-Jurgen Koch/Minden Pictures; page 15, inset: © Dwight Kuhn Photography; page 16: © Heidi & Hans-Jurgen Koch/Minden Pictures; page 17: © Heidi & Hans-Jurgen Koch/Minden Pictures; page 18: © Heidi & Hans-Jurgen Koch/Minden Pictures; page 19: © Getty Images; page 19, inset: © Getty Images; page 20: © Dwight Kuhn Photography; page 21: © Corbis; page 22: © DK Limited/Corbis; page 22, inset: © Ullstein-Klein/Peter Arnold, Inc.; page 24: © DK Limited/Corbis ©; back cover: © Tom McHugh/Photo Researchers Inc.

Photo research by Dwayne Howard
Design by Holly Grundon

12 11 10 9 8 7 6 5 4   9 10 11 12/0

Printed in China
First printing, March 2007

Contents

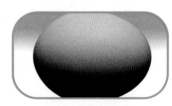

Chapter 1

Chicks and Chickens

Cheep, cheep! Cluck, cluck! This book will tell you all about chicks and chickens.

rooster

hen

chicks

A baby chicken is called a chick. An adult female chicken is called a hen and an adult male chicken is called a rooster.

These pictures show seven breeds of chickens. How is each one different?

Buff Brahma

White Leghorn

Derby Red Cap

Not all chickens look the same. There are more than 100 breeds of chickens in the world.

White-Lace Red Cornish

Silver Campine

Dominique

New Hampshire Red

All of the chickens in one breed have feathers with the same color and pattern.

Parts of a Chicken

tail feathers

comb

beak

wattle

wing

claw

This picture shows the main parts of an adult chicken. Chickens have feathers and wings, but they cannot fly very far. They get around by walking.

Both hens and roosters have red combs and wattles. But chickens do not start out looking this way. Let's learn about their life cycle to see how they grow and change!

Chapter 2

An Egg Is Laid

See this hen? She is laying an egg! Most hens lay one or two eggs a day.

If an egg has not been **fertilized**, then a chick does not grow inside. These are the eggs we eat for breakfast.

If the egg has been fertilized by a rooster, a chicken begins to grow inside.

Inside the Egg

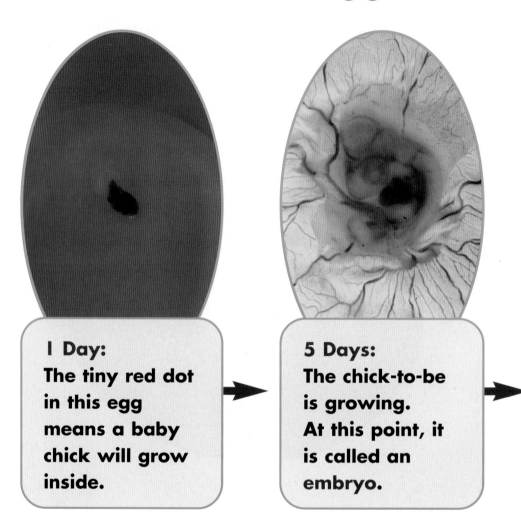

1 Day:
The tiny red dot in this egg means a baby chick will grow inside.

5 Days:
The chick-to-be is growing. At this point, it is called an embryo.

Let's take a peek inside a fertilized egg.

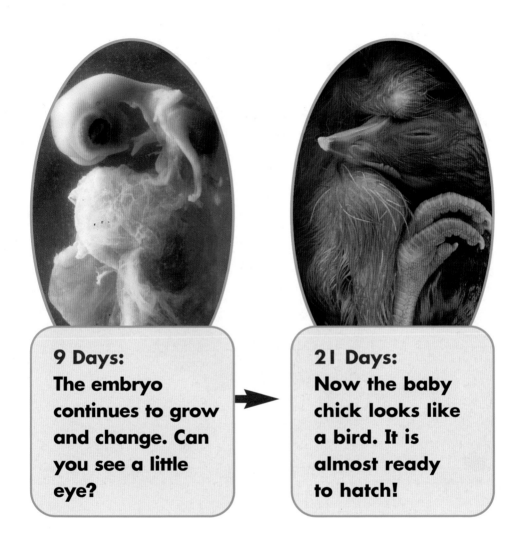

9 Days:
The embryo continues to grow and change. Can you see a little eye?

21 Days:
Now the baby chick looks like a bird. It is almost ready to hatch!

It takes about three weeks for the egg to develop into a chick.

Chapter 3

Time to Hatch

A hen sits on her eggs until it's time for them to hatch. She keeps them nice and warm. This is called **incubation**.

Fast Fact

The lump on a chick's beak is called an **egg tooth.**

When a chick is ready to be born, it uses its egg tooth to break through the shell.

Peck, peck, peck! The chick pecks small holes
around the egg. Then it uses its head to push
open the shell.

Fast Fact

It takes most chicks about five
hours to hatch from their eggs.

The chick keeps pecking and pushing.
At last, the tired chick is out of its egg.
Welcome to the world!

Chapter 4

Growing Up

When a chick is first born, it doesn't look so cute. It is very wet and very sticky.

A group of newborn chicks is called a brood.

But soon the feathers dry and become fluffy. This yellow fluff is called **down**.

Fast Fact

Chicks eat feed, which is a mixture of grains. It helps them grow strong.

The new chick explores the world with its mother and fellow chicks. There is much to discover!

The little chick gets bigger and bigger.
It learns how to make a cheeping sound.
This helps the chick's mother to find it.

A five-month-old female chicken is old enough to lay eggs.

In a few weeks, the chick sprouts feathers and a tiny red comb and wattle. In a few months, it will be all grown-up. Egg-cellent!

Glossary

breed (breed): a particular type of animal

brood (brewd): a group of newborn chicks

comb (kohm): bright red skin on top of a chicken's head

down (doun): the soft feathers of a bird

egg tooth (eg tooth): a sharp bump on the end of a newborn chick's beak

embryo (em-bree-oh): an animal in its earliest stage of development

feed (feed): a mix of grains that chicks eat

fertilize (fur-tuh-lize): when reproduction begins

incubation (ing-kyuh-bay-shuhn): eggs are kept warm until they are ready to hatch

wattle (wot-uhl): red skin under a chicken's beak

Comprehension Questions

1. Can you name and describe two parts of a grown-up chicken?

2. Can you share two facts about a chick that is growing inside an egg?

3. Can you share two facts about a chick that is hatching from an egg?

4. Can you think of two words to describe a chick?

Bonus Chicken Jokes

Q. What did the egg do when the hen told it a joke?

A. It cracked up!

Q. Why did the chick's beak break?

A. Because it was cheep!